EMMA BLAND SMITH • Illustrated by JENN ELY

THE GARDENER OF ALCATRAZ

A TRUE STORY

ini Charlesbridge

For my brothers, Michael, Alastair, and Andrew Bland, my partners
in crime growing up in San Francisco—E. B. S.

For Wonderful Rio—J. E.

I would like to thank the following people for helping me with the research:
Shelagh Fritz, Michael Esslinger, Corrina Gould, Gerry Wright, and Adrian Baker.—E. B. S.

Published by Charlesbridge
9 Galen Street, Watertown, MA 02472 • (617) 926-0329
www.charlesbridge.com

Library of Congress Cataloging-in-Publication Data
Names: Smith, Emma Bland, author. | Ely, Jenn (Jennifer Kristin), 1983– illustrator.
Title: The gardener of Alcatraz: a true story / Emma Bland Smith; illustrated by Jenn Ely.
Description: Watertown, MA: Charlesbridge, 2022. | Audience: Ages 7–10. |
    Audience: Grades 2–3. | Summary: "When prisoner Elliott Michener began
    tending the gardens at Alcatraz, his thoughts of escape were replaced with new
    skills and a sense of dignity. Back matter discusses the history of Alcatraz and
    the US prison system today."—Provided by publisher.
Identifiers: LCCN 2020052037 (print) | LCCN 2020052038 (ebook) |
    ISBN 9781623541606 (hardcover) | ISBN 9781632899453 (ebook)
Subjects: LCSH: Michener, Elliott | United States Penitentiary, Alcatraz Island,
    California—Biography—Juvenile literature. | Prisoners—United States—
    Biography—Juvenile literature. | Gardeners—California—Alcatraz Island—
    Biography—Juvenile literature. | Gardens—California—Alcatraz Island—
    Juvenile literature.
Classification: LCC HV9474.A53 S65 2022 (print) | LCC HV9474.A53 (ebook) |
    DDC 364.1092 [B]—dc23
LC record available at https://lccn.loc.gov/2020052037
LC ebook record available at https://lccn.loc.gov/2020052038

Printed in China
(hc) 10 9 8 7 6 5 4 3 2 1

Illustrations done in gouache and digital
Display font set in Din Slab Serif by Sandra Winter, Tom Grace, and Akira Kobayashi
Text type set in Futura by Paul Renner and Minion Pro Condensed by Robert Slimbach
Color separations and printing by 1010 Printing International Limited in Huizhou,
    Guangdong, China
Production supervision by Jennifer Most Delaney
Designed by Cathleen Schaad

The boat chugged out of San Francisco and into the bay. Sound nice? It wasn't. This was no pleasure outing, let me tell you.

Gulls squawked. A foghorn moaned. And Elliott Michener, prisoner #AZ-578, stared into the fierce wind. Ahead loomed an island topped with a concrete fortress, watchtowers, and barbed wire.

Alcatraz.
The toughest prison in the country.

As the twenty new inmates marched off the boat, Elliott felt full of dread. How had things gone so wrong?

Five years ago, he'd had life figured out, printing counterfeit money. But making fake money was a crime. He'd been sent to the slammer—first in Kansas, now here, at Alcatraz.

Surrounded by water and steel bars, Elliott saw nothing but gray.

There was no way he was staying here. He'd bust out and go back to counterfeiting or maybe rob a bank.

Sure, security was tight on Alcatraz. No prisoner had ever managed to escape.

But Elliott was smart. Maybe he'd be the exception.

Outdoor Life 15¢

As the days crawled by, he lay low. He endured the no-talking rules. He avoided the riots. He performed his dreary job, scouring the ground for handballs that had been knocked over the rec yard wall.

Make no mistake: it was a tedious life.

Until the day when, so they say, Elliott stumbled across something that was most definitely not a handball.

A key.

Elliott could have kept the key, tried it in every gate on the island. Why didn't he? Between you and me, he was probably scheming. He figured that if he did something honest, something you might not expect from a prisoner, it could pay off.

So instead, he handed over that key.
And our story takes a turn.

11

Because, see, it just so happened that the big bosses on Alcatraz were looking for an inmate to help with the gardens, which sorely needed attention. Of course, it couldn't be just anyone. It had to be someone honest, someone they could trust with a little extra independence. Someone who would, say, turn in a key.

Elliott got the job.

Now, Elliott didn't know a darn thing about plants. But he figured this job had to be better than picking up handballs.

His first task was breaking up the soil on the island's west side and creating terraces. He threw himself into it.

Gardening wasn't half bad. It was hard, satisfying work. Elliott decided he might as well get good at it.

What's more, this job could be his ticket to freedom. The gardens were outside the prison walls. Elliott found a quiet spot where the guards couldn't see him and started building a contraption that he hoped would allow him to swim to shore.

Once he was tinkering with some rubber tubing when a guard surprised him. Elliott croaked something about it being a sprinkling device. The guard swallowed the story hook, line, and sinker. Phew.

Elliott finished the terraces. He learned which plants went where, and how much to water them. He was too busy to focus on his flotation device.

As time passed, a funny thing happened. This gardening thing started to grow on him. He studied seed packets and books from the prison library. He built a greenhouse and tried out composting. He even created his own narcissus hybrid.

Elliott Michener planted every square inch of the island that he could!

Color spread from outdoors to in. Prisoners picked flowers to put in their water glasses.

To get supplies, Elliott would talk a guard into buying him seeds or bulbs in the city. In exchange Elliott would slip the guard some flowers for his wife.

Elliott didn't think much about escaping anymore.

Seven years passed. By now Elliott had gotten such a good reputation that he was promoted to work for Warden Swope and his wife in their home. Swell!

His official job was keeping the house tidy and cooking the meals. But in his free time, he kept on gardening. This jailbird, you see, had grown an honest-to-goodness green thumb.

Mrs. Swope liked gardens, too. The dignified lady and the tough Alcatraz inmate became friends. She loved roses, and he was happy to grow them for her.

The two unlikely friends listened to the radio together, and they both enjoyed horse racing. They followed the races and cheered for their favorites. On Elliott's birthday Mrs. Swope gave him a new pair of shoes.

After a while Elliott was taking care of the house for days at a time when the Swopes went away. They trusted him and treated him like a person, and that made life on Alcatraz bearable.

The island had changed in the nine years since Elliott had arrived. The gray was gone. In its place was green. And other colors! Pink snapdragons. Red geraniums. Purple iris.

Elliott, too, had changed. He knew sedum from sage and dahlias from daffodils. He also had passion, pride, and solid skills. He could see a colorful future for himself—one that didn't involve breaking the law.

And here is where our story takes another turn. One morning Elliott got some unexpected news.

He was leaving Alcatraz! He was going to Leavenworth, a lower-security prison! Wouldn't you think he'd be pleased as punch?

TRANSFER

- 578 -

Nope.

Believe it or not,
Elliott begged to stay in
Alcatraz, the toughest prison
in the country.

But he had no choice. He packed
his gardening manuals. And though color
bloomed all around him, once again he saw
nothing but gray.

The boat chugged toward the city. And Elliott Michener, prisoner #AZ-578 no longer, stared into the fierce wind as he left the island he had helped transform.

Leavenworth was bleak. There were no gardening jobs for prisoners.

Elliott was desperate to get out. He knew what he had to do.

Escape? No, sir. He stayed on his best behavior, kept out of trouble, and asked to get out early.

33

And get out early he did.

When Elliott was released for good behavior, he went to work on a farm in Wisconsin. For the first time in ages, he could breathe fresh air and grow his beloved flowers. Once more color filled his life.

Elliott never went back to crime. Gardening had, sure enough, been his ticket to freedom. Just not in the way he'd expected.

And Then What Happened?

In Leavenworth Prison, in Kansas, Elliott Michener was actually homesick for Alcatraz, where he had been a prisoner from 1941 to 1950. He wrote to Warden Swope in 1951: "I believe that my best and only practical course is to get back to Alcatraz. . . . At Alcatraz I could at least grow Bell roses and delphiniums seven days a week and enjoy considerable freedom and trust."

Happily, after two years of good behavior, he was paroled on a dairy farm in Wisconsin, where his counterfeiting buddy Dick Franseen was already working. The two former partners in crime worked hard, determined to prove how much they had changed. As Elliott wrote to the parole board, "You may rest assured that we're going to live GOOD lives." Their employer was fond of them both and seemed to trust them completely.

Elliott never forgot the kindness of Mr. Swope, who had advocated for his early parole. They corresponded frequently, the warden often addressing Elliott as "My dear Michener."

In one of his letters, Elliott wrote, "I'm learning how much better one can do living honestly than by, say, counterfeiting!" And then, before signing off, the tough guy turned gardener added one more thing. He asked the warden for a very special favor. Could he and Dick possibly have a cutting of their favorite Alcatraz rose?

After several years of impeccable parole reports, Elliott was permitted to move on. In Southern California he married and led a productive life. "It continually amazes me that so many good things have happened," he wrote to Mr. Swope. "Ain't that sumpin'?"

According to one source, Elliott became a landscaper later in his life, putting his gardening skills to good use. He passed away in 1997.

A report from around the time Elliott arrived in Alcatraz called him a "habitual and confirmed criminal of a most dangerous and vicious type." He was said to be highly intelligent but antisocial, with no attachment to anyone.

Photo courtesy of the National Archives at San Francisco.

Alcatraz and Its Gardens

The Early Years

Until the mid-1800s, Alcatraz was a rocky, barren island in San Francisco Bay. Because there was no source of water, Native people did not live on the island (although historians believe that members of the Ohlone tribe may have hidden there to avoid being captured and forced into slavery in the California Mission system).

Beginning around 1850 the US military began to develop the island as a fort from which to protect the bay and growing city. Prisoners were held there, too. By 1861 Alcatraz had officially become a military detention center, imprisoning soldiers accused of crimes. Native Americans were also imprisoned there for refusing to allow their children to be taken away and placed in boarding schools.

For the next sixty years, military families called the island home. In an effort to make it more livable, they imported soil from nearby Angel Island and brought in seeds and plants. By 1933, when the military left, the island was home to wildflowers, trees, and even a charming Victorian cottage garden.

In gardening, Elliott found something to care about. As he later explained, "The hillside provided a refuge from the disturbances of the prison, the work a release, and it became an obsession. This one thing I would do well."

Photo courtesy of Golden Gate National Recreation Area, Park Archives (GOGA 2316-83-C-4).

Alcatraz Federal Penitentiary

The island entered its notorious phase as a federal penitentiary in 1934. This was the era of Prohibition, when the law banned the sale of alcohol. Organized criminal networks sold alcohol on the black market, which led to an explosion of crime. Suddenly there were many more people behind bars. The government wanted a new maximum-security, "escape-proof" prison for the toughest of the tough. Infamous crime boss Al Capone was, in fact, one of the first inmates sent to Alcatraz.

Although most depictions of Alcatraz feature primarily white inmates, there were some people of color as well. In all, the island housed 1,252 white prisoners, 282 Black prisoners, and smaller numbers of Asian, Latino, and Native people. As was common in many parts of the United States during this time, racial segregation was, shamefully, the rule in many situations on Alcatraz.

Security on Alcatraz was high. The smallest infraction could send an inmate to solitary confinement. Bribery was not tolerated. No newspapers were allowed. Inmates *were* allowed to borrow books from the library and play instruments, handball, and softball.

Reviving the Gardens—with Help

Freddie Reichel, the secretary to the first Alcatraz warden, decided to bring the neglected gardens back to life. He sought help from horticulturist Kate Sessions, who famously transformed San Diego's Balboa Park, and embraced the use of native species and low-water plants.

But the island was too big for one person. With much effort Reichel persuaded the authorities to let inmates help. Some prisoners, like Elliott Michener, took to this new job with growing passion.

Elliott later wrote that working in the gardens provided a welcome relief from the close confines of the prison. He planted every square inch he had access to and became increasingly devoted to his job. Under his care poppies cascaded down hills. Seedlings sprouted in the greenhouses. Elliott even persuaded prison officials to let inmates save bathwater for the plants. He went from knowing nothing to being an expert gardener.

Elliott proved so trustworthy that after seven years, he was promoted to household help for the new warden, Edwin Swope, and his wife, Edna. In this position Elliott flourished even more.

A Closer Look at Inmate Gardening

In Alcatraz the relative freedom that came with a gardening job improved prisoners' morale and outlook. While they transformed the island, gardening changed them.

Before he became a gardener, Elliott was assigned to tasks such as picking up handballs and doing laundry. He did not find these jobs remotely fulfilling. As a gardener, Elliott got to use not only his body but also his brain. He was clearly intellectually stimulated, and he went above and beyond the expectations of the job. (He even took a correspondence class in biology from Pennsylvania State College.)

Today experts know that giving incarcerated people meaningful work is

Elliott shared a love of roses with Edna Swope, the wife of the warden. Here he poses with the Swopes' dog outside their Alcatraz home.
Photo courtesy of Golden Gate National Recreation Area, Park Archives (GOGA 2316-83-C-2).

important and worthwhile. Gardening in particular has been shown to be a therapeutic pastime that improves inmates' quality of life. Inmates who are trained in gardening are also less likely to return to prison. They develop skills they may be able to use on the outside.

However, we also now realize that prison labor raises serious ethical questions. Many inmates are forced to work for free or for very low wages. The prison system benefits from their labor, as do consumers who purchase goods produced by inmates. The exploitation of people in prison is a troubling practice that we all need to look at more closely.

Another important question is whether Elliott's relative privilege as a white inmate influenced the opportunities he was afforded. Would prisoners of color have been given the chance to work in the gardens and the warden's house, positions that were considered elite? Most likely no, due to deeply ingrained racism and bias. We admire prisoners who take steps to change their lives, yet the playing field is often not level from the start.

The Native Occupation

As time passed, Alcatraz proved far too expensive to maintain. The government decided to close the prison and transferred the last prisoners out in March 1963. For the next

few years, the buildings stood empty and the gardens fell into neglect.

Then, in 1969, a group of Native activists from different tribes occupied Alcatraz. Their goal was to raise awareness about the brutal ways in which Native people had been treated and to protest the recent closings of reservations across the country. The Indians of All Tribes occupied Alcatraz for nineteen months before the government evicted them. Signs of their presence remain on the island to this day, inspiring visitors to reflect upon Indigenous people's ongoing fight for their rights.

The Alcatraz Gardens Today

The island was taken over by the National Park Service in 1972. In 2003 two nonprofit agencies (the Garden Conservancy and the Golden Gate National Parks Conservancy) combined forces to begin restoration of the gardens. Today more than two hundred species of plants flourish on the island! Some of the roses that Elliott tended for Mrs. Swope still exist, and two of the greenhouses have been rebuilt on their original foundations. The lush landscape is the legacy of the prisoner gardeners of Alcatraz Island—and a metaphor for the resilience of the human spirit.

Some of the Alcatraz gardens today, restored to their former glory. Photo copyright © by Elizabeth Byers.

"I am grateful for my introduction to the spade and the trowel, the seed and the spray can. They have given me a lasting interest in creativity."
—Elliott Michener

Author's Note

Researching this book involved many people and processes. I was excited to find valuable and revealing primary sources, such as prison reports on Elliott Michener, a recorded audio interview, and a delightful exchange of letters between Elliott and Warden Swope.

Several experts reviewed the book for accuracy. Shelagh Fritz, the Program Manager for the Alcatraz gardens, read the story many times and looked closely at the depictions of plants. Corrina Gould, Tribal Chair of the Confederated Villages of Lisjan, went over the passages concerning Native people's relationship with Alcatraz. Michael Esslinger, author of *Alcatraz: A History of the Penitentiary Years*, answered myriad questions; verified details about uniforms, prison layout, and more; and shared stories of his real-life meeting with Elliott.

Jenn Ely and I tried to be as accurate as possible in both text and art. In rare cases, we took light artistic license. For example, in reality, inmates arriving at Alcatraz would have been inside the cabin of the boat. In the crucial opening scene, we decided to show Elliott on deck so readers could see his face.

Although Elliott's story is a hopeful one, the whole team and I agreed that our goal was to avoid presenting a falsely rosy view of prison life. We strove to show the people behind the black-and-white photos, while not minimizing crime or downplaying the harshness of Alcatraz.

Selected Bibliography

Primary Sources

Alcatraz Island staff. Conduct record for Elliott Michener, 1941–1944.

Alcatraz Island staff. Signed record of Elliott Michener's belongings taken upon transfer to Leavenworth, Nov. 16, 1950.

Alcatraz Island staff. Special progress report on Elliott Michener, July 16, 1948.

Landrum, C. U. Letter from US Attorney to Alcatraz parole board, Sept. 19, 1950.

Leavenworth Penitentiary staff. Admission summary of Elliott Michener, date unclear but likely 1939.

Leavenworth Penitentiary staff. Physical and mental evaluation of Elliott Michener, Aug. 2, 1939.

Leavenworth Penitentiary staff. Transcript of interview with Elliott Michener after his escape attempt from Leavenworth, July 24, 1941.

Michener, Elliott. Letter to Golden Gate National Park Service, Sept. 11, 1982.

Michener, Elliott. Letter to Judge James Johnston, Feb. 19, 1952.

Michener, Elliott. Letters to Edwin Swope, 1951–1954.

Michener, Elliott. Oral history, Sept. 7, 1995.

Reichel, Freddie. Letter to the California Horticultural Society, date unknown but likely 1977.

Reichel, Freddie. Letter to Evelyn Strong, Alcatraz, 1977.

Swope, Edwin. Letters to Elliott Michener, 1950–1954

Ward, Charles. Letter to Edwin Swope, Nov. 24, 1950.

Books

Esslinger, Michael. *Alcatraz: A History of the Penitentiary Years*. San Francisco, CA: Ocean View, 2016.

Hart, John. *Gardens of Alcatraz*. San Francisco, CA: Golden Gate National Park Association, 1996.

Wellman, Gregory. *A History of Alcatraz Island, 1953–2008*. Charleston, SC: Arcadia, 2008.

Online Resources

Barclay, Eliza. "Prison Gardens Help Inmates Grow Their Own Food—and Skills." NPR, Jan. 12, 2014. https://www.npr.org/sections/thesalt/2014/01/12/261397333/prison-gardens-help-inmates-grow-their-own-food-and-skills.

Golden Gate National Park Conservancy. "The Gardens of Alcatraz." www.alcatrazgardens.org.

National Park Service. "The Fascinating History of Alcatraz Island." Last updated Feb. 12, 2020. www.nps.gov/alca/learn/historyculture/index.htm.

DVD

Epps, Kevin. *The Black Rock: AKA Black Alcatraz*. Mastamind Productions: National Park Service, 2009.

For a full bibliography, visit www.emmabsmith.com.